CELEBRATE CHRISTMAS

*Holiday & Inspirational
Songs & Poems*

By
Lauri Allen

AuthorHouse™
1663 Liberty Drive
Bloomington, IN 47403
www.authorhouse.com
Phone: 1-800-839-8640

First published by AuthorHouse 07/20/2011

ISBN: 978-1-4567-1332-4 (sc)
ISBN: 978-1-4567-1333-1 (ebk)

Library of Congress Control Number: 2010917853

Printed in the United States of America

TABLE OF CONTENTS

HOLIDAY SONGS

INSPIRATIONAL SONGS

HOLIDAY SONGS & POEMS

(Poem) ALL YEAR LONG IT'S CHRISTMAS FOR THE CHILDREN

AND THE ANGELS SPOKE

ANNIE & WILLIE'S PRAYER
A Christmas Story-Song
(Adapted from a Poem by Sophia P. Snow)

A TWENTIETH CENTURY CHRISTMAS

CHRISTMAS IN YOUR HEART EVERY DAY

(Poem) TIME FOR CHANGE

CHRISTMAS IS FOR SINGLES TOO

FAMILY AND FRIENDS

LITTLE THINGS

LULLABY FOR THE ANIMALS

(Poem) SEASONS

ONCE-IN-A-YEAR TIME THING

SHINE (Like the Colors of Christmas)

SING HIM A BRAND NEW SONG

SING OF JOY

THE GIFT OF LOVE

(Poem) TRADITION

THE SMALLEST ANGEL
A Christmas Story-Song

'TIS THE SEASON

YESTERDAY'S HOLIDAYS

(Poem) WHAT IS IT?

FORWARD

Whatever you believe,
We each have a heart and we function the same as human beings.
Whatever your birth place,
Your traditions came with you to celebrate in harmony with those of this,
Our home land, America.

As a new country,
America welcomed everyone from other lands,
Including the beliefs that they brought with them.
We never said they had to forsake their beliefs or worship in a certain way.
We only established laws to live by in this land for the good of all
So that we could continue to enjoy the freedom of believing
However we chose.
We must not destroy that freedom for the sake of a few
Who wish to oppose or twist the meaning of the laws of this land.
This will only serve to divide us.

In the old countries,
Tradition was that important adhesive underlying the unity of a people.
America welcomed all traditions
And that, in itself, became a tradition to be celebrated.
Our traditions came from ancient times,
All lands and from all societies.
In whatever forms we have brought them to this land,
And for the good of our unity,
Even as we evolve as a society,
We need to recognize and celebrate all of our traditions.

Lauri Allen
December 2005

FORWARD

Whatever you believe,
We each have a heart and we function the same as human beings.
Whatever your birth place,
Your traditions came with you to celebrate in harmony with those of this,
Our home land, America.

As a new country,
America welcomed everyone from other lands,
Including the beliefs that they brought with them.
We never said they had to forsake their beliefs or worship in a certain way.
We only established laws to live by in this land for the good of all
So that we could continue to enjoy the freedom of believing
However we chose.
We must not destroy that freedom for the sake of a few
Who wish to oppose or twist the meaning of the laws of this land.
This will only serve to divide us.

In the old countries,
Tradition was that important adhesive underlying the unity of a people.
America welcomed all traditions
And that, in itself, became a tradition to be celebrated.
Our traditions came from ancient times,
All lands and from all societies.
In whatever forms we have brought them to this land,
And for the good of our unity,
Even as we evolve as a society,
We need to recognize and celebrate all of our traditions.

Lauri Allen
December 2005

HOLIDAY SONGS & POEMS

(Poem) <u>ALL YEAR LONG IT'S CHRISTMAS FOR THE CHILDREN</u>

AND THE ANGELS SPOKE

ANNIE & WILLIE'S PRAYER
A Christmas Story-Song
(Adapted from a Poem by Sophia P. Snow)

A TWENTIETH CENTURY CHRISTMAS

CHRISTMAS IN YOUR HEART EVERY DAY

(Poem) <u>TIME FOR CHANGE</u>

CHRISTMAS IS FOR SINGLES TOO

FAMILY AND FRIENDS

LITTLE THINGS

LULLABY FOR THE ANIMALS

(Poem) <u>SEASONS</u>

ONCE-IN-A-YEAR TIME THING

SHINE (Like the Colors of Christmas)

SING HIM A BRAND NEW SONG

SING OF JOY

THE GIFT OF LOVE

(Poem) <u>TRADITION</u>

THE SMALLEST ANGEL
A Christmas Story-Song

'TIS THE SEASON

YESTERDAY'S HOLIDAYS

(Poem) <u>WHAT IS IT?</u>

ALL YEAR LONG, IT'S CHRISTMAS FOR THE CHILDREN

All year long, it's Christmas for the children.
Every day can fill them with surprise.
Morning sunlight can excite them;
Change of season will delight them
And the colors of a rainbow fill their eyes.

All year long, it's Christmas for the children.
They see his brightest star shine every night.
They hear his voice in all the music of the earth;
In songs and laughter heard since their time of birth
And their bedtime stories always turn out right

And when the celebrated day arrives,
The child in everyone contrives
To make it brighter, longer, richer and more full
Than any day of the year before,
Whether a school day or a weekend to explore,
Whether Spring or Sumjer or this time of Yule.

Each dawn is new, a birth and life for living,
And every joy and tear will hold thanksgiving
Through work and play, through sleep and dreams
Whether glad or sad or other extremes,m
All year long or just this season,
For the children, any day's a reason not to wait,
But to step right up, dance, sing and celebrate!

By Lauri Allen
December 2003

AND THE ANGELS SPOKE

Bethlehem's Innkeeper gave them to stay
A place in the stable, a bed made of hay.
And Joseph and Mary, whom heaven had led,
Brought Jesus, the sweet babe, to lay.

And the Angels spoke and the star shone bright
Peace on earth, good will to men this night.

Here came the shepherds who followed the star,
They and three Wise Men who came from afar.
All heard the music and voices above
Sang sweetly to show them the way.

And the Angels spoke and the star shone bright,
Peace on earth, good will to men this night.

Joy to the world, He was born on this eve;
Christ is the Lord and let all men believe.
Let all who would know and abide in His name
Find love in their hearts on this day.

Then the word was spread through the heavenly night,
And the Angels spoke, Allelujah.
Then the word was spread through the heavenly night,
And the Angels sang, Allelujah.

C 1976

AND THE ANGELS SPOKE

BY LAURI ALLEN (A.S.C.A.P.)

ANNIE AND WILLIE'S PRAYER
Adapted from a Poem by Sophia P. Snow

'T'was the eve before Christmas; "Goodnight" had been said
And Annie and Willie crept into bed.
There were tears on their pillows and tears in their eyes
And each little bosom was heaving with sighs;
For tonight, their stern father's command had been given;
That they should retire precisely at seven
Instead of at eight, for they troubled him more
With questions unheard of ever before.

He had told them he thought this delusion a sin;
No such creature as "Santa Claus" ever had been
And he hoped after this, he should never more hear
How he scrambled down chimneys with presents each year.
And this was the reason that two little heads
So restelessly tossed on their soft, downy beds.
Eight, nine, and the clock on the steeple tolled ten;
Not a word had been spoken by either till then...

When Willie's sad face from the blanket did peep
And whispered, "Dear Annie, is 'ou fast as'eep?
"Why, no, brother Willie" a sweet voice replies.
I've long tried in vain, but I can't shut my eyes,
For somehow, it makes me so sorry because...
Dear Papa has said there is no Santa Claus.
Now, we know there is, and it can't be denied,
For he came ev'ry year before Mamma died.
But then, I've been thinking that she used to pray
And God would hear everything Mamma would say.

And maybe she asked Him to send Santa Claus here
With that sackful of presents he brought every year.
"Well, why tant we p'ay, dest as Mamma did den
And ask Dod to send him with presents aden?
"I've been thinking so, too" and without a word more,
Four little bare feet bounded out on the floor,
And four little knees, the soft carpet pressed,
And two tiny hands were clasped close to each breast.
"Now, Willie, you know, we must firmly believe
That the presents we ask for we're sure to receive;

6

"Dear Jesus, look down on my brother and me
And grant us the favor we're asking of thee.
I want a wax dolly, a tea set and ring,
An ebony workbox that shuts with a spring.
Bless Papa, dear Jesus, and cause him to see
That Santa Claus loves us as much as does he.
Don't let him get fretful and angry again
At dear brother Willie and Annie, Amen!

"Please, Desus, 'et Santa Taus tum down tonight
And b'ing us some p'esents before it is light.
I want he should div' me a nice 'ittle s'ed
With bright shinin' 'unners and all painted red;
A box full of candy, a book and a toy,
Amen, and den, Desus, I'll be a good boy."

They were lost soon in slumber, both peaceful and deep
And with fairies in dreamland were roaming in sleep.

Eight, nine, and the little french clock had struck ten;
'Ere the father had thought of his children again.
"I was harsh with my darlings" he mentally said
"And should not have sent them so early to bed.
But then, I was troubled; my feelings found vent,
For bank stock today has gone down ten percent.
But of course, they've forgotten their troubles ere this
And that I denied them the thrice-asked-for kiss.

But just to make sure, I'll go up to their door,
For I never spoke harsh to my darlings before.
So saying, he softly ascended the stairs
And arrived at the door to hear both of their prayers.
"Strange, strange, I'd forgotten, " said he with a sigh
"How I longed, when a child, to have Christmas draw nigh.
I'll atone for my harshness" he inwardly said,
"By answering their pray'rs ere I sleep in my bed."

Then he turned to the stairs and softly went down,
Threw off the velvet slippers and silk dressing gown,
Donned hat, coat and boots and was out on the street,
A millionaire facing the cold driving sleet.
Nor stopped he until he had bought everything
From the box full of candy to the tiny gold ring.

Indeed, he kept adding so much to his store
That the various presents outnumbered a score.
Then homeward he turned, when his holiday load
With Aunt Mary's help, in the nurs'ry was stowed.

And as the fond father, the picture surveyed,
He thought for his trouble, he had amply been paid.
I've enjoyed more pure pleasure than ever before;
What care I if bank stock falls ten percent more!
Hereafter, I'll make it a rule, I believe,
To have Santa Claus visit us each Christmas Eve."
So thinking, he gently extinguished the light
And tripping downstairs, retired for the night.
As soon as the beams of the bright morning sun
Put the darkness to flight and the stars, one by one,
Four little blue eyes out of sleep opened wide
And at the same moment, the presents espied.

They laughed and they cried in their innocent glee
And shouted for Papa to come quickly and see
What presents old Santa Claus brought in the night;
(Just the things that they wanted) and left before light.
"And now," added Annie, in a voice soft and low,
"You'll believe there's a Santa Claus, Papa, I know."
While dear little Willie climbed up on his knee,
Determined no secret between them should be,
And told, in soft whispers, how Annie had said
That their dear blessed Mamma so long ago dead
Used to kneel down by the side of her chair
And that God up in Heaven had answered her pray'r.

"Den we dot up and prayed, dust as well as we tould,
And Dod answered our prayers, now wasn't he dood?
"I should say that he was if he sent you all these
And knew just what presents my children would please."
("Well, well, let him think so, the dear little elf;
'T'would be cruel to tell him I did it myself.")

Blind father, who caused your stern heart to relent
And the hasty words spoken so soon to repent?
'T'was the being who bade you steal softly upstairs
And made you his agent to answer their prayers.

ANNIE AND WILLIE'S PRAYER

Adapted from a Poem by
SOPHIA P. SNOW

Music By
LAURI ALLEN (A.S.C.A.P.)

4.

Emi7   A   F   Fma7   Eb   Dmi7   Dbma7

ASK-ING OF THEE__ I WANT A WAX DOL-LY__ A TEA-SET AND RING__ AN
_FORE IT IS LIGHT__ I WANT HE SHOULD DIV' ME__ A NICE 'IT-TLE S'ED__ WITH
PRE-SENTS ES-PIED__ THEY LAUGHED AND THEY CRIED IN THEIR IN-NO-CENT GLEE__ AND
TWEEN THEM SHOULD BE__ AND TOLD IN SOFT WHIS-PERS HOW AN-NIE HAD SAID__ THAT THEIR

C7   Bb/C   Fma7

EB-O-NY WORK-BOX THAT SHUTS WITH A SPRING__ BLESS PA-PA__ DEAR
BRIGHT SHIN-IN' 'UN-NERS AND ALL PAINT-ED RED__ A BOX__ FULL OF
SHOUT-ED FOR PA-PA__ TO COME QUICK AND SEE__ WHAT PRE- SENTS OLD
DEAR BLESS-ED MAM-MA__ SO LONG A-GO DEAD__ USED__ TO KNEEL

Ebma7   Dmi7   Dbma7   C   F   Dmi7

JE- SUS__ AND CAUSE HIM TO SEE _____ THAT SAN-TA CLAUS LOVES US AS
CAN- DY__ A BOOK AND A TOY _____ A-
SAN- TA CLAUS BROUGHT IN THE NIGHT _____ (JUST THE THINGS THAT THEY WANT-ED) AND
DOWN BY THE SIDE OF HER CHAIR _____ AND THAT GOD UP IN HEAV-EN__ HAD

Gmi7   Gmi7/C   Fma7   Ebma7   Dmi7

MUCH AS DOES HE __DON'T LET HIM GET FRET-FUL AND AN-GRY A-GAIN__
LEFT BE-FORE LIGHT. "AND NOW" ADD-ED AN- NIE IN A VOICE SOFT AND LOW__
AN-SWERED HER PRAY'R. "DEN WE DOT UP AND PRAYED__ DUST WELL AS WE TOULD__

Dbma7   C   F   Dmi7   Gmi7   Gmi7/E   A7/E   1ST X

_____ AT DEAR BRO-THER WIL-LIE AND AN-NIE__ A- MEN!" (2) PLEASE
_____ "YOU'LL BE-LIEVE THERE'S A 'SAN-TA CLAUS' PA-PA__ I KNOW.__ (4) WHILE (2ND X) al
_____ AND DOD AN-SWERED OUR PRAY-ERS NOW__

Bbma7   Ami7   Abma7   Gmi   Gmi7/C

CODA
__ MEN__ AND THEN__ DE-JUS__ I'LL BE A DOOD BOY." THEY WERE__

12

5.

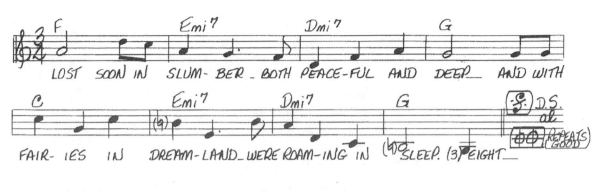

LOST SOON IN SLUM-BER _ BOTH PEACE-FUL AND DEEP_ AND WITH

FAIR-IES IN DREAM-LAND _ WERE ROAM-ING IN (4) SLEEP. (3) EIGHT_

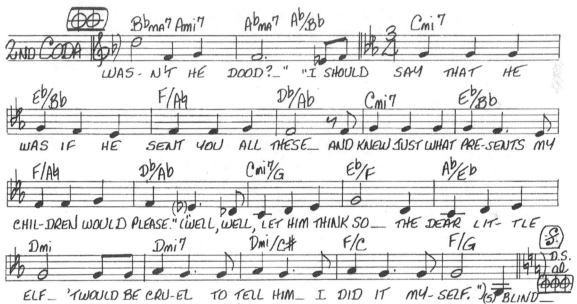

2ND CODA

WAS-N'T HE DOOD?_" "I SHOULD SAY THAT HE

WAS IF HE SENT YOU ALL THESE_ AND KNEW JUST WHAT PRE-SENTS MY

CHIL-DREN WOULD PLEASE." ("WELL, WELL, LET HIM THINK SO_ THE DEAR LIT-TLE

ELF_ 'TWOULD BE CRU-EL TO TELL HIM_ I DID IT MY-SELF.")(5) BLIND_

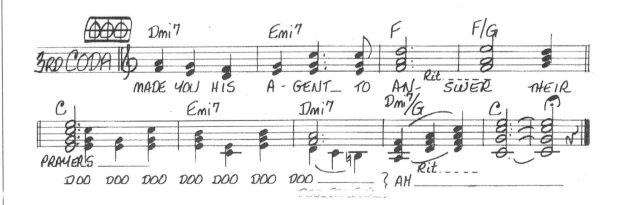

3RD CODA

MADE YOU HIS A-GENT_ TO AN-SWER THEIR

PRAYERS_

DOO DOO DOO DOO DOO DOO DOO_ ? AH_

A TWENTIETH CENTURY CHRISTMAS

Once again, the weather has turned cold.
Neighborhoods aglow with colored lights,
All the stores show red and green and gold,
Crowds of shoppers checking out the sights.

Lots of Santas hear the children's wishes.
They've been good and sure deserve the best.
We buy gifts on credit so judiciously,
What T.V. Commercials have stressed.

It's a Twentieth Century Christmas;
A holiday season of today.
A Twentieth Century Christmas;
It isn't like yesterday,
And what'll we have to pay
tomorrow?

Bright-eyed kids crowd screens to watch the action.
Once they might have asked for skates or bikes.
Now, electric games are the attraction;
Genesis, Nintendo and the likes.
Pinetree topped sedans travel the freeways.
Parties offer eggnog and buffet.
Drive-by shootings give us little lee-way,
So, police are out in force each holiday.

Dobbin doesn't pull our sleigh today;
To visit Grandma, we must take a jet.
All across the nation, our traditions' blown away;
Now our future's in debt.
No more do we give token gifts of love.
Unemployment leads to push and shove, you know,
In and economic spiritual plateau.

It's a Twentieth Century Christmas;
A holiday season of today.
A Twentieth Century Christmas;
It isn't like yesterday,
And after each Christmas Day,
We're gonna have to pay for tomorrow!

C 1992

A TWENTIETH CENTURY CHRISTMAS

BY LAURI ALLEN (A.S.C.A.P.)

2.

CODA ... F/A ... G ... Em Em7/D A/C# A7

(4) __ LICE ARE OUT IN FORCE EACH HOL-I- DAY_____

D (BRIDGE) B7 ... Em7 ... A7

DOB-BIN DOES-N'T PULL OUR SLEIGH TO-DAY____ TO VIS-IT GRAND-MA WE MUST TAKE A

D7 ... Dm7 ... G ... E ... Am7

JET____ ALL A-CROSS THE NA-TION OUR TRA-DI-TION'S BLOWN A-WAY, OUR FU-TURE'S IN

Fm7 ... G ... Dm7/G ... C/G

DEBT____ UN-EM-PLOY-MENT LEADS TO PUSH AND SHOVE ____ NO

G ... Gm ... Gm/C ... D.S. al

MORE DO WE GIVE TO-KEN GIFTS OF LOVE ____ IT'S A __

2ND CODA Db+/Gb ... Bb7/F ... Bb7/C

AF-TER EACH CHRIST-MAS DAY__ WE'RE GON-NA HAVE TO PAY__ FOR TO-
ritard ____

Gm7 Gb7 F7

_ MOR-ROW ____

16

CHRISTMAS IN YOUR HEART EVERY DAY

Merry Christmas,
Have a very Merry Christmas.
Give a part of you to someone new
And it's Christmas in your heart every day.

There's good reason
To be happy every season,
'Cause the love is there for you to share
With some Christmas in your heart every day.

It's such a little thing,
But a smile can bring a tear of joy and warmth untold.
And a hand to hold on Christmas Eve
Makes the winter cold just make believe
And there's no reason why you can't try
To give some love away every day.

So, Merry Christmas,
Give your heart away this Christmas.
Everywhere you go, let someone know
That it's Christmas in your heart every day.
Make it Christmas in your heart...
Every day.

C 1979

CHRISTMAS IN YOUR HEART
EVERY DAY

BY LAURI ALLEN (A.S.C.A.P.)

2.

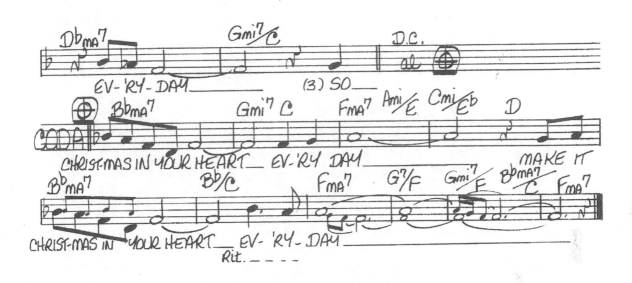

EV-'RY-DAY _____ (3) SO _____

CHRIST-MAS IN YOUR HEART_ EV-'RY DAY _____ MAKE IT

CHRIST-MAS IN YOUR HEART_ EV-'RY-DAY _____
Rit. _ _ _ _

TIME FOR CHANGE

In cycles, seasons come and go,
Their love so briefly sweet.
Through warmth and wet,
Color and cold,
Not lasting long enough to grow old,
They live, ever youthful,
Fade at their peak,
And sleep till next heartbeat,
For it's only life they seek.

So should we, live youthfully,
Become each season,
Ageless and true,
Reflect and rest in Winter's view.
And let Spring culminate its ride.
From Summer rain,
Morning dew,
Through falling leaves,
From trees changing hue,
And we...
Love and free the child inside.

December 1998

CHRISTMAS IS FOR SINGLES TOO!

Chestnuts roasting; good cheers toasting, presents under the tree.
Carol singing and sleighbells ringing;
It's really a fantasy.

Snowflakes falling, good friends calling to celebrate His time of year.
A time to treasure, but where's the pleasure
In loneliness as a career?

Christmas isn't only for families.
Christmas isn't only for children and friends.
It shines on lonely folk too, on singles alone, stressed out and blue.
Christmas isn't only for families.
For giving and making amends.
His star is up there too, for each single anew, guiding them through,
Yes, Christmas is for singles too.

Christmas shopping, tree-lot hopping to find the bargains and sales.
Christmas trimming and good cheer brimming
Over the top of the scales.

Yes, it's a jolly time of hustle and bustle and stress,
Spending extra time and money can make your life a mess;
Putting up the tree and hanging outside lights,
Overwork and office parties leads to lonely nights...
And a runny cold, with no one to hold you!

And then, it's New Year's Eve.
You think you've had your fling.
And you can make believe all you'll achieve;
Toast your champagne and sing... to being single!

Christmas isn't only for families.
Christmas isn't only for children and friends.
It shines on lonely folk too too, on singles alone, stressed out and blue.
Christmas isn't only for families,
For giving and making amends.
His star is up there too, for each single anew, guiding them through,
Yes, Christmas is for singles too!

C 1986

CHRISTMAS IS FOR SINGLES TOO

BY LAURI ALLEN (A.S.C.A.P.)

YES___ CHRIST-MAS IS FOR SING-LES___

100 _____

SCALES___ YES IT'S A JOL-LY TIME OF HUST-LE AND

BUS-TLE AND STRESS__ SPEND-ING EX-TRA TIME AND MON-EY CAN MAKE YOUR LIFE A MESS___

PUT-TING UP THE TREE___ AND HANG-ING OUT-SIDE LIGHTS___ O-VER-WORK AND OFF-ICE PAR-TIES

LEADS TO LONE-LY NIGHTS___ AND ___A RUN-NY COLD_____ WITH NO ONE TO

HOLD___ YOU___ AND THEN IT'S NEW YEAR'S EVE_____ YOU

THINK YOU'VE HAD YOUR FLING___ AND YOU CAN MAKE-BE-LIEVE___ ALL YOU'LL A-

CHIEVE__ TOAST YOUR CHAM-PAGNE AND SING___ TO BE-ING SING-LE

23

3.

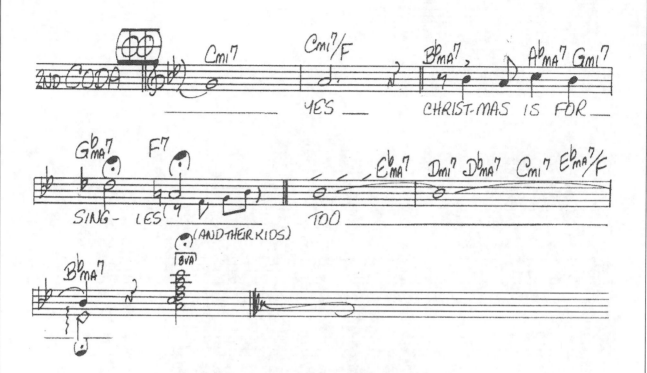

Cmi7 ... **Cmi7/F** YES ... **Bᵇma7**, **Aᵇma7 Gmi7** CHRIST-MAS IS FOR

Gᵇma7 **F7** SING- LES (AND THEIR KIDS) **Eᵇma7 Dmi7 Dᵇma7 Cmi7 Eᵇma7/F** TOO

Bᵇma7 (BVA)

FAMILY AND FRIENDS

The days are getting shorter,
The atmosphere is light.
Thanksgiving dinner's now digested,
Holiday season's now in sight.
The shops and malls are all aglow
With cheer and colored lights
And bustling shoppers interested in
Finding gifts just right...

For the Family and Friends.
They're everything that makes life worthwhile.
Family and Friends,
When you're down and blue, nothing comforts you
Like just knowing where there are folks who care
On whom your life depends:
Family and Friends.

As the season's weather changes,
Sunny days give way to rain.
Though snow is white, its cold may bite
And your health may sometimes not sustain.
And if you're feelin' lonely
And there's no way left to go,
Just send word and you'll be heard...
Reach out and say hello...

To the Family and Friends;
They're everything that makes life worthwhile.
Family and Friends,
When you're down and blue, nothing comforts you
Like just knowing where there are folks who care
On whom your life depends:
Family and Friends.

C 1991

FAMILY AND FRIENDS

BY LAURI ALLEN (A.S.C.A.P.)

1. THE DAYS___ ARE GET-TING SHORT-ER___ THE AT-MOS-PHERE IS LIGHT___
2. AS THE SEA- SON'S WEATH-ER CHANG-ES___ SUN-NY DAYS GIVE WAY TO RAIN___

THANKS-GIV-ING DIN-NER'S NOW___ DI-GEST-ED___
THOUGH SNOW IS WHITE___ ITS COLD___ MAY BITE___ AND YOUR

HOL-I-DAY SEA-SON'S NOW IN SIGHT___ THE SHOPS AND MALLS ARE ALL A-GLOW___ WITH
HEALTH___ MAY SOME-TIMES NOT SUS-TAIN AND IF YOU'RE FEEL-IN' LONE-LY___ AND THERE'S

CHEER AND COL-ORED LIGHTS___ AND BUST-LING SHOP-PERS IN-
NO WAY LEFT TO GO___ JUST___ SEND WORD AND YOU'LL

___TER-EST-ED IN FIND-ING GIFTS JUST RIGHT___ FOR THE
___BE HEARD___ REACH OUT AND SAY HEL-LO___ TO THE

FAM-I-LY___ AND FRIENDS___ THEY'RE EV'-RY-THING THAT MAKES LIFE WORTH-WHILE

FAM-I-LY___ AND FRIENDS___ WHEN YOU'RE DOWN AND BLUE___

NOTH-ING COM-FORTS YOU___ LIKE JUST KNOW-ING WHERE THERE ARE

© 1994

26

2.

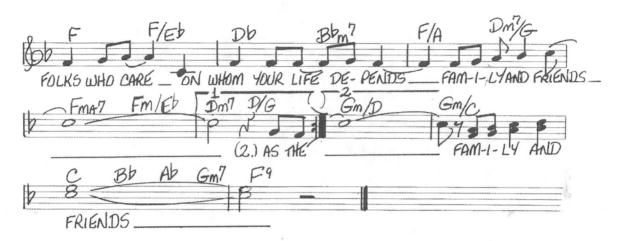

F   F/Eb   Db   Bbm7   F/A   Dm7/G

FOLKS WHO CARE __ ON WHOM YOUR LIFE DE-PENDS ___ FAM-I-LY AND FRIENDS __

Fma7   Fm/Eb   1. Dm7 D/G   2. Gm/D   Gm/C

_____ (2.) AS THE _____ FAM-I-LY AND

C   Bb   Ab   Gm7   F9
8

FRIENDS _____

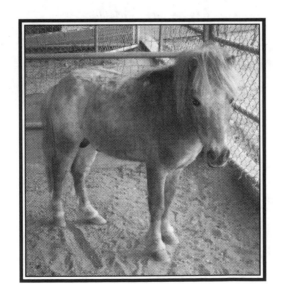

LITTLE THINGS

Little Things, Little Things, Little Things...

A steaming cup of cocoa,
A fireplace glowing bright,
Whole neighborhoods dressed in festive lights
That twinkle through the night.

Everyone feels more friendly;
People let down their guards
To visit next door or down the block
And bring their best regards.

Little things bring comfort, little things bring joy.
You don't have to win the lottery to please ev'ry girl and boy.
Little things make mem'ries to think of all next year.
Little things mean love of life
And to all mankind good cheer.

Laughter becomes infectious;
There's holiday games and song
And people who never raise their voices
Are singing right along.

Put out the holiday candles,
The holly, the tree and train;
Each time that toy train falls off the track,
You patiently put it back.

Little things bring comfort, little things bring joy.
You don't have to win the lottery to please ev'ry girl and boy.
Little things make mem'ries to think of all next year.
Little things mean lofe of life
And to all mankind, good cheer.

The memories
Of little things like these
Promise a happy and healthy New Year.

C 1993

LITTLE THINGS

BY LAURI ALLEN (A.S.C.A.P.)

INTRO: FMA7 ... Dm7 ... BbMA7 ... /C

LIT-TLE THINGS___ LIT-TLE THINGS___ LIT-TLE THINGS___

FMA7 ... Eb/F ... Bb

1. A STEAM-ING CUP OF CO-COA___ A FIRE-PLACE GLOW-ING BRIGHT___
2. LAUGH-TER BE-COMES IN-FEC-TIOUS___ THERE'S HOL-I-DAY GAMES AND SONG___

Bbm(MA7) Bb6 ... F ... Am7/E ... AbMA7/Eb

___ WHOLE NEIGH-BOR-HOODS DRESSED IN FES-TIVE LIGHTS___ THAT
AND PEO-PLE WHO NEV- ER RAISE THEIR VOI-CES___ ARE

Gm7/D ... Gm7/C ... FMA7

TWIN-KLE THROUGH THE NIGHT___
SING-ING RIGHT A - LONG___ EV- 'RY-ONE FEELS MORE
PUT OUT THE HOL-I-DAY

Eb/F ... Bb ... Bbm(MA7) Bb6 ... F ... Am7/E

FRIEND-LY___ PEO-PLE LET DOWN THEIR GUARDS___ TO VIS-IT NEXT DOOR OR
CAN-DLES___ THE HOL-LY, THE TREE AND TRAIN___ EACH TIME THAT TOY TRAIN FALLS

AbMA7/Eb ... Gm7/D ... Fm/C ... Bb7

DOWN THE BLOCK AND BRING THEIR BEST RE-GARDS. ___
OFF THE TRACK YOU PA-TIENT-LY PUT IT BACK___

2.

30

LULLABY FOR THE ANIMALS

Sleep little ones.
Sleep and watch your dreams.
Sandman is calling you to his arms
On this bright Christmas night.

Sleep safely together,
Under the soft moonbeams.
Father looks over you from above
On this bright Christmas night.

Sweet little souls, pure and naïve,
Love is your mission in all you achieve.
Sleep now and wake to the light
Shining on you Christmas morning bright.

But sleep, now, sweet ones.
Dream of your food and play.
Helping those you love is your life
In the morning's light,
In the sun so bright.

So, sleep, now, little ones.
Morning's not far away.
May you never know hunger or strife.
Father looks over you from above,
Shining upon you eternal love;
Christmas Day will waken you to His skies of blue,
So sleep now,
Go deep now,
And dream.

C 2010

LULLABY FOR THE ANIMALS

BY LAURI ALLEN (A.S.C.A.P.)

SEASONS

In Spring our sweet earth rain
Fills each new life that breathes and blooms.
It feeds and nurtures,
Mother, Father to us all.

Summer's sun replenishes,
Exhilarates and urges us to play,
Plan new life and reach high,
Stand straight and tall.

Autumn loves us most of all,
Blankets life in beauty, silent, pure and clear,
Calling forth a dormant fire to stir the chronicler
And awaken the adventurer.

In Winter's dreams, the most ingenious seeds begin,
And not yet crystaline,
Evolve prophetic, cabaline.

Every season perennial does recall
The birth, child, growth and death of all,
Enchanting, arcane!
Mystical!

December 1996

ONCE–IN–A–YEAR–TIME THING
(Christmas)

Snowflakes falling, friends a-calling, presents to buy for all.
Why don't we do it in April or June,
Carve up a turkey on May's full moon.
Practice good will from midnight to noon?
It's a once-in-a-year-time thing,
Christmas.

Carol singing, church-bells ringing, Heavenly music fills all.
Why can't we hear it in Summer or Fall,
Mail greeting cards at the robin's first call,
Decorate a tree for a Valentine Ball?
It's a once-in-a-year-time thing,
Christmas.

Why can't we show our love all through the year?
Like little children do, spreading good cheer?
From nation to country, from city to town,
From neighbor to friends and fam'ly on down to yourself?

And if you don't like yourself,
Your love grows dusty on a shelf,
Like a book that's unread, so the words go unsaid.
It's a chain that grows longer
And generations stronger,
And every year in December,
Suddenly, we remember
How to love... how to love... how to love;
It's a once-in-a-year-time thing,
A once-in-a-year-time fling,
Christmas.

Hot drinks brewing, eggnogs cooling, parties welcoming all.
Why don't we party the whole year through,
Love one another, no matter who,
Celebrate the seasons the same way too?
And once a year, at the most, play host,
And raise your glass and toast
The New Year!

C 1990

35

ONCE-IN-A-YEAR TIME THING
(CHRISTMAS)

BY LAURI ALLEN (A.S.C.A.P.)

DON'T LIKE YOUR-SELF, YOUR LOVE GROWS DUS-TY ON A SHELF_ LIKE A BOOK THAT'S UN-READ_ SO THE

WORDS GO UN-SAID__ IT'S A CHAIN THAT GROWS LONG-ER_ AND GEN-ER-A-TIONS STRONG-ER_ AND

EV'-'RY YEAR_ IN DE-CEM-BER ___ SUD-DEN-LY WE RE-MEM-BER_ HOW TO.

LOVE_____ HOW TO LOVE_____ HOW TO

LOVE_____ IT'S A ONCE-IN-A-YEAR TIME THING___ A

ONCE-IN-A-YEAR-TIME FLING_ CHRIST-MAS.___

SAME WAY TOO_ AND_ONCE A YEAR, AT THE MOST_ PLAY HOST_ AND

RAISE YOUR GLASS AND TOAST_ THE NEW YEAR!

SHINE
(Like The Colors of Christmas)

Red is for holly berries frosty and bright.
Saint Nick in red is a Christmas delight.
Red balls tinkle upon the tree
And little red lips laugh when they wake up and see it all...

Shine like the stars do on Christmas Eve.
Shine like the eyes of each beautiful soul.
Shine like the sunlight on Christmas Day.
Shine every day,
Make it your goal.

Green is the mistletoe placed just out of sight.
Green is the holly wreath hanging just right.
Green Christmas tree dressed in tinsel and gold
Warms each heart from young to old when they see it all...

Shine like the stars do on Christmas Eve.
Shine like the eyes of each beautiful soul.
Shine like the sunlight on Christmas Day.
Shine every day,
Make it your goal.

Silv'ry White Angel on top of the tree;
Silv'ry white snowflakes of lace falling free
And they shine for you and me.

Shine like the stars do on Christmas Eve.
Shine like the eyes of each beautiful soul.
Shine like the sunlight on Christmas Day.
Shine every Christmas,
You can too, just for you,
Shine!

C 1981

SHINE
(LIKE THE COLORS OF CHRISTMAS)

BY LAURI ALLEN (A.S.C.A.P.)

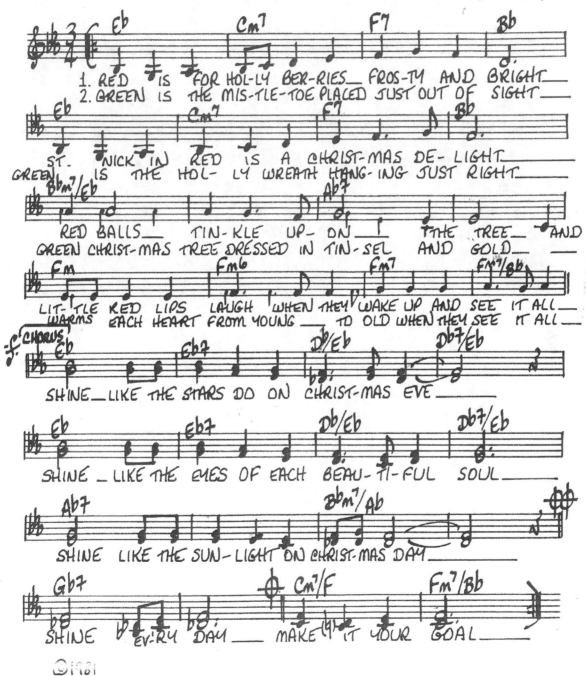

1. RED IS FOR HOL-LY BER-RIES FROS-TY AND BRIGHT
2. GREEN IS THE MIS-TLE-TOE PLACED JUST OUT OF SIGHT

ST. NICK IN RED IS A CHRIST-MAS DE-LIGHT
GREEN IS THE HOL-LY WREATH HANG-ING JUST RIGHT

RED BALLS TIN-KLE UP-ON THE TREE AND
GREEN CHRIST-MAS TREE DRESSED IN TIN-SEL AND GOLD

LIT-TLE RED LIPS LAUGH WHEN THEY WAKE UP AND SEE IT ALL
WARMS EACH HEART FROM YOUNG TO OLD WHEN THEY SEE IT ALL

CHORUS
SHINE LIKE THE STARS DO ON CHRIST-MAS EVE

SHINE LIKE THE EYES OF EACH BEAU-TI-FUL SOUL

SHINE LIKE THE SUN-LIGHT ON CHRIST-MAS DAY

SHINE EV-'RY DAY MAKE IT YOUR GOAL

© 1981

2.

CODA

Cm⁷/F   F7   [BRIDGE] Gb7

MAKE IT YOUR GOAL__ SIL-V'RY WHITE AN-GEL ON

Ab/Bb   Bb7   Eb   Eb7

TOP OF THE TREE__ SIL-V'RY WHITE SNOW-FLAKES OF

Cm⁷   Cm⁷/F   Bb

LACE FALL-ING FREE__ AND THEY SHINE__ SHINE__ FOR__

Gm⁷   Fm⁷

YOU__ FOR YOU__ AND ME__

Fm⁷/Bb   D.S. al

2No CODA   Gb7   Cm⁷/Bb   Fm⁷/Bb

SHINE EV-'RY CHRIST-MAS__ YOU CAN__ TOO__ JUST FOR__

Bb7   Eb   Eb7   Db7/Eb   Ab7

YOU__ SHINE__ SHINE__ SHINE__

Bbm⁷/Ab   Cm⁷/F   SHINE__ Fm⁷/Bb   Eb7

SHINE__ JUST FOR YOU__ opt. SHINE__

40

SING HIM A BRAND NEW SONG

Sing Him a brand new song,
Sing Him a brand new song,
A song of today.
Let the bells ring out and the trumpets play,
Let your praises shout, He is here to stay,
Sing Him a brand new song of today.

He gave us night, gave us day,
And He's here to show us the way,
With a heavy load through the darkest night
On the longest road, we can follow his light back home.

He gave us land, gave us sea,
And a heart that longs to be free,
Like the stars on high, and the rivers flow,
Like the birds that fly, we are sure to be going home.

Sing Him a brand new song,
Sing Him a brand new song,
A song of today.
Let the bells ring out and the trumpets play,
Let your praises shout, He is here to stay,
Sing Him a brand new song of today.

He gave us life, gave us love,
And a soul to keep us above
Every earthly care and our man-made schemes,
If we learn to share, we can follow our dreams back home.

He gave us joy, gave us tears,
And he took away all our fears.
With a loving hand and a smiling face,
Made us understand, we can follow his grace back home.

Sing Him a brand new song,
Sing Him a brand new song,
A song of today.
Let the bells ring out and the trumpets play,
Let your praises shout, He is here to stay,
Sing Him a brand new song
Of today.

C 1978

SING HIM A BRAND NEW SONG

BY LAURI ALLEN (A.S.C.A.P.

SING OF JOY

It's that special time of year,
When the streets are filled with cheer
In anticipation of a holiday.
When fam'lies gather 'round to raise their happy sound
In Christmas carols solemn, sweet and gay.

And they sing of joy
And glory to God,
And love and peace, good will to all mankind.
Each girl and boy sings glory to God,
Look toward the morrow and the happiness we'll find.

Then it's gone before we know,
And the years, they come and go
Without anticipating any joy at all.
But watch the children through the year,
Seems they're always filled with cheer
And a joy that comes with Summer, Spring or Fall.

And they sing of joy, and glory to God,
And love and peace, good will to all mankind.
Sing of joy and glory to God;
Look toward the morrow and the happiness we'll find.

Where is the child in me all year long?
Why does it sleep till mid-December?
Where is the child in me that loves the whole year long?
Why can't I wake him and take him through the whole year
With love and peace and cheer?

And sing of joy and glory to God,
And love and peace, good will to all mankind.
Sing of joy and glory to God,
Look toward the morrow and happiness we'll find.
Let's sing of joy and glory to God,
And love and peace, good will to all mankind...
Let's sing of joy!

C 1981

43

SING OF JOY

BY LAURI ALLEN (A.S.C.A.P.)

1. It's that spe-cial time of year __ when the streets are filled with cheer __
2. Then it's gone be-fore we know __ and the years they come and go __

In an-ti-ci-pa-tion of a hol-i-
With-out an-ti-ci-pa-ting an-y joy at

Day __ when fam-'lies gath-er 'round __ to
All __ but watch the chil-dren thru the year __ seems they're

Raise their hap-py sound __ in Christ-mas car-ols
Al-ways filled with cheer __ and a joy that comes __ with

Sol-emn, sweet and gay __ and they sing of __
Sum-mer, spring or fall __

(CHORUS)
Joy __ and glor-y to God __ and love and peace good will __

To all man-kind __ Each girl and sing of __

Boy __ sings glor-y to God __ look to-ward the mor-
Joy __ and

44

2.

___ROW___AND THE HAP-PI-NESS WE'LL FIND_____ (2) THEN IT'S

HAP-PI-NESS WE'LL FIND_____ WHERE IS THE CHILD__

__IN {ME / US} ALL YEAR LONG__WHY DOES IT SLEEP TILL MID-DE-CEM-

__BER____ WHERE IS THE CHILD__IN ME__THAT LOVES THE

WHOLE YEAR LONG__ WHY CAN'T I WAKE HIM AND TAKE HIM__THRU THE

WHOLE YEAR__WITH LOVE AND PEACE AND CHEER__AND SING OF__

3.

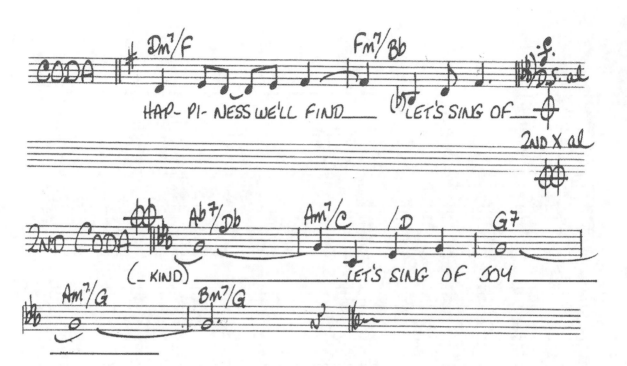

CODA · Dm⁷/F · · · · Fm⁷/Bb · · · D.S. al f.

HAP-PI-NESS WE'LL FIND___ (b)LET'S SING OF___

2ND X al

2ND CODA · Ab⁷/Db · Am⁷/C · /D · G7

(_ KIND)___ LET'S SING OF JOY___

Am⁷/G · Bm⁷/G

THE GIFT OF LOVE

Just the hint of a grin brings the warmth right in.
Just the softest touch lets you feel so much.
And the glow of that welcome feeling shining all around,
Lifts you off the ground at Christmas.

Maybe one short call or a neighbor's "How y'all",
Or an open door held by one who walked before you
Gives you such a lift with all that happiness around,
How can you be down at Christmas with the gift of Love?

Oh, it's shining, sending it's message through the air,
Loud and clear, everywhere,
You can hear the joyous sound ringing above.
Every cheering, endearing, uplifting thought,
And the kindnesses brought to each heart
Mean a lot more than you'd think;
Raise your glasses and drink
To the gift of love.

So, if your message is soft, it'll carry to the loft.
With the greatest of ease, not a soul you won't please.
Take a baby step and you'll be leaping to the sky,
How your sparks will fly,
Just say, "Hi, Merry Christmas".
It's the gift of love.

Oh, it's shining, sending it's message through the air,
Loud and clear, everywhere,
You can hear the joyous sound ringing above.
Every cheering, endearing, uplifting thought
And the kindnesses brought to each heart
Mean a lot more than you'd think;
Raise your glasses and drink
To the gift of love;
To the gift of love.

C 1985

THE GIFT OF LOVE

BY LAURI ALLEN (A.S.C.A.P.)

JUST THE HINT OF A GRIN BRINGS THE WARMTH RIGHT IN JUST THE SOFT-EST TOUCH LETS YOU FEEL SO MUCH AND THE GLOW OF THAT WEL-COME FEEL-ING SHIN-ING ALL A-ROUND LIFTS YOU OFF THE GROUND AT CHRIST-MAS IT'S THE GIFT OF LOVE (2) MAY-BE ONE SHORT CALL OR A NEIGH-BOR'S "HOW Y'ALL" OR AN O-PEN DOOR HELD BY ONE WHO WALKED BEFORE YOU GIVES YOU SUCH A LIFT WITH ALL THAT HAP-PI-NESS A-ROUND HOW CAN YOU BE DOWN AT CHRIST-MAS WITH THE GIFT OF LOVE OH IT'S

TO THE GIFT OF LOVE

TRADITION

When the leaves turn red and gold and crackle 'neath your feet
And the winds turn colder, swirling as they blow,
Then the season takes over and emotions compete
With memories, regrets and good wishes aglow.

When the fat man in the red suit makes the children's eyes bright,
And the comfort of old carols warms your heart to the core,m
And a tree with all the trimmings lights windows in the night,
We can celebrate the differences from each folklore.

When family and friends call up to say hi or are just dropping by
Bringing gifts brightly wrapped that they hope you'll adore,
And the eggnog and hot choc'late warms to satisfy,
It's a holiday high; you couldn't wish for more.

Can you feel it?
Do you get it?
It's that time again.
It's tradition at its highest filling us with joy
And a love we can't destroy,
Making us proud we are countrymen.

Can we keep it?
Never lose it?
Throughout each year?
It's tradition at its highest filling us with love,
Straight to you from above
And 't'will only make us stronger,
Undivided, living longer.
Can we try? Persevere?
Every day, every week, keep it up through the year?
Don't deny
Your Tradition.

December 2005

51

THE SMALLEST ANGEL
A Christmas Story-Song

A tear rolled to rest on the freckle-tipped nose
of a four-year old's fearful but defiant pose.
Then he swung on the gate, as they entered his name
And from that moment on, Heaven wasn't the same.

His halo was tarnished, a-tilt over-head;
His ear-splitting whistle inspired much dread.
His feather-fine wing-tips, he nervously bit
And his shrill, off-key voice put the Heavenly choir in a snit.

He was the smallest Angel with the tiniest wings,
Too busy playing to take care of things.
A mischievous cherub in sweet, childish play;
He tried to be good for the Lord, his God;
He tried to be good for the Lord.

'T'was certain he needed some discipline soon,
Before he tried tossing or bouncing the moon.
So the Angel of Peace took him up on his knee,
Asking "What earthly home-sickness cure could there be?"

"There's a box I left back home under my bed."
"You shall have it!" he nodded, and a messenger sped
To bring back the box to Paradise,
To gladden and brighten the smallest Angel's sad eyes.

He was the Smallest Angel with the tiniest wings;
Too busy playing to take care of things.
From that moment on, with great joy in his heart,
He was such a good boy for the Lord, his God;
He was such a good boy for the Lord.

Glad tidings soon spread; Paradise was a hive,
For Jesus, God's Son, was soon to arrive.
And all Heaven's host was preparing his due;
But what could the Smallest Angel do?

He couldn't compose a lyrical hymn
Or write a new pray'r for the cherubim.
For musical talent, he greatly did yearn
And his literate skill, he lamentably had yet to learn.

Oh, what could he give? There was just one thing;
His box of earth treasures for the blessed Earth King.
But amongst all the glorious gifts resplendent,
He knew his was shabby, unworthy, irreverent.

Too late to retrieve it, God's hand came to rest
On the Smallest Angel's small, unsightly wood chest.
Weeping hot bitter tears, he turned and fled,
But he stumbled when suddenly, the voice of God said:

(Spoken)
Of all the Angels' precious gifts,
With this small box I am most pleased.
Its contents are of earth and men
And my Son is born King of both of these.
He, too, will know and love these things,
And when his task is done, He will leave them.
I accept this gift for Jesus, born of Mary this night, in Bethlehem.

And what earthly treasures had he saved inside?

A golden-winged butterfly, once flying free,
Two white stones from a muddy river bank,
A sky-blue egg from a nest in an olive tree,
And a limp, leather collar, worn by his dog
Whose soul was in heaven and now was free.

(Sung)
Then the wooden box glowed with an unearthly light
And became a lustrous flame, such a radiant sight.
Then he saw it rise up like a beckoning gem.
The Smallest Angel's lowly gift
Was the shining star of Bethlehem.

He was the Smallest Angel with the tiniest wings
And in between playing, his sweet soul sings.
The treasure he owned was the love in his heart
And he gave all he had to the Son of God;
Yes, he gave all he had to the Lord.

C 1987

53

THE SMALLEST ANGEL

BY LAURI ALLEN (A.S.C.A.P.)

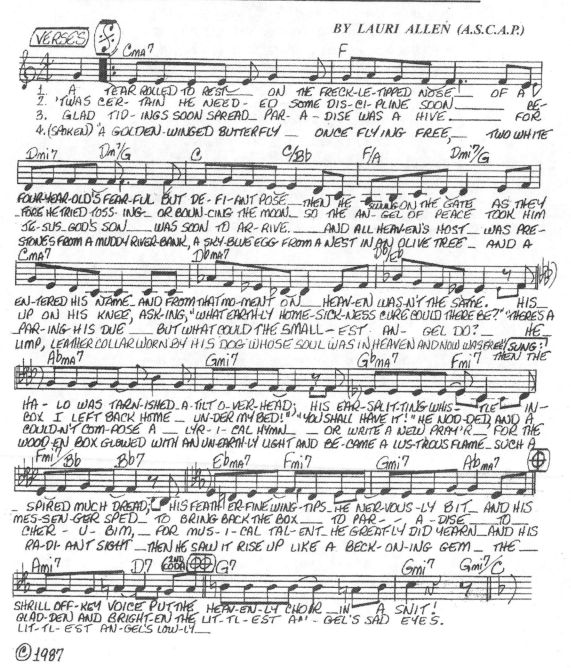

2.

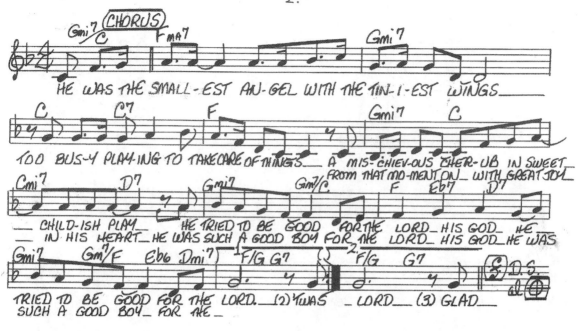

HE WAS THE SMALL-EST AN-GEL WITH THE TIN-I-EST WINGS___

TOO BUS-Y PLAY-ING TO TAKE CARE OF THINGS___ A MIS-CHIEV-OUS CHER-UB IN SWEET___
FROM THAT MO-MENT ON___ WITH GREAT JOY

___ CHILD-ISH PLAY___ HE TRIED TO BE GOOD FOR THE LORD___ HIS GOD___ HE
___ IN HIS HEART___ HE WAS SUCH A GOOD BOY FOR THE LORD___ HIS GOD___ HE WAS

TRIED TO BE GOOD FOR THE LORD.___ (2) TWAS___ LORD___ (3) GLAD___
SUCH A GOOD BOY___ FOR THE___

LIT-ER-ATE SKILL___ HE LA-MENT-A-BLY HAD YET TO LEARN.___ OH___

(1) WHAT COULD HE GIVE? THERE WAS JUST ONE THING___ HIS BOX OF EARTH TREA-SURES FOR THE
(TOO) (2) LATE TO RE-TRIEVE IT___ GOD'S HAND CAME TO REST ON THE SMALL-EST AN-GEL'S SMALL, UN-

BLESS-ED EARTH KING___ BUT___ A-MONGST ALL THE GLOR-I-OUS GIFTS___ RE-SPLEN-DENT HE
___SIGHT-LY WOOD CHEST___ WEEP-ING HOT BIT-TER TEARS___ HE TURNED AND FLED___ BUT HE

KNEW HIS WAS SHAB-BY___ UN-WORTH-Y IR-REV-'RENT___ (1) TOO___

STUMB-LED WHEN SUD-DEN-LY___ THE VOICE OF GOD SAID:___

3.

(SPOKEN): "OF ALL THE ANGELS' PRECIOUS GIFTS___ ___ WITH THIS SMALL BOX___ I AM MOST PLEASED___ ___ ITS CONTENTS ARE OF ___EARTH AND MEN AND___

MY SON IS BORN KING OF BOTH OF THESE. ___HE TOO WILL KNOW AND ___ LOVE THESE THINGS___ ___ AND WHEN HIS TASK IS DONE___ ___ HE WILL LEAVE THEM.

I ACCEPT THIS GIFT FOR JESUS___ BORN OF MARY THIS NIGHT IN BETHLEHEM."

(SPOKEN): AND WHAT EARTHLY TREASURES HAD HE SAVED INSIDE?

___ GIFT WAS THE SHIN-ING STAR OF BETH-LE-HEM. ___

HE WAS THE SMALL-EST AN-GEL WITH THE TIN-I-EST WINGS___ AND

IN BE-TWEEN PLAY-ING___ HIS SWEET SOUL SINGS___ THE TREA-SURE HE OWNED WAS THE LOVE___

___ IN HIS HEART___ AND HE GAVE ALL HE HAD TO THE SON OF GOD___YES, HE___

GAVE ALL HE HAD___ TO THE LORD.

'TIS THE SEASON

'Tis the season, so they say
When the elves come out to play.
With their leader, old Kris Kringle,
Work and fun begin to mingle.
Fa-la-la, La-la-la-la-la.

Spirits lift and hearts feel light,
Like the stars a-winter night.
Carolers can't resist a song
They've rehearsed all year long.
Tra-la-la, La-la-la.

'Tis the season overflowing with good will.
'Tis the season every heart will have its fill.
And the reason for this rebirth every year
Is to keep the flame of love burning bright
And to hold the gift of life dear in sight
And to be of good cheer at this holiday time of the year.

Busy stores stay open late
For those fam'lies shopping late.
Sparkling snowflakes softly falling,
Friends and neighbors come a-calling.

'Tis the season best of all,
'Tis the season, deck the hall
For one and all.

C 1991

'TIS THE SEASON

BY LAURI ALLEN (A.S.C.A.P.)

1. 'TIS THE SEA-SON__ SO THEY SAY__ WHEN THE ELVES COME
2. SPIR-ITS LIFT AND__ HEARTS FEEL LIGHT__ LIKE THE STARS A-
3. BUS-Y STORES STAY__ O-PEN LATE__ FOR THOSE FAM-'LIES

OUT TO PLAY__ WITH THEIR LEAD-ER__ OLD KRIS KRING-LE__
__WIN-TER NIGHT__ CAR-OL-ERS CAN'T RE- SIST A SONG__
SHOP-PING LATE__ SPARK-LING SNOW-FLAKES SOFT-LY FALL-ING__

WORK AND FUN BE- GIN TO MIN-GLE__ FA-LA-LA
THEY'VE RE-HEARSED IT ALL YEAR LONG__
FRIENDS AND NEIGH-BORS COME A-CALL-ING__

LA LA LA LA LA__

TRA-LA LA LA LA LA 'TIS THE SEA-SON O-VER-

__FLOW-ING WITH GOOD WILL __ 'TIS THE SEA-SON__ EV-'RY

HEART WILL HAVE ITS FILL.__ AND THE REA-SON FOR THIS

RE-BIRTH EV- 'RY YEAR __ IS TO KEEP THE FLAME OF LOVE BURN-ING

© 1991

58

2.   "'TIS THE SEASON"

BRIGHT____ AND TO HOLD THE GIFT OF LIFE DEAR IN SIGHT____ AND TO

BE OF GOOD CHEER____ AT THIS HOL-I-DAY TIME OF THE

YEAR.____

CODA 'TIS THE SEA-SON BEST OF ALL____

'TIS THE SEA-SON, DECK THE HALL____ FOR ONE AND____

ALL.____

YESTERDAY'S HOLIDAYS

It's a time to remember, reflect and recall
Old days and good friends, the best times of all.
And thanks for remembering
Helps to celebrate this season of holidays.

Visit family and neighbors and call those afar;
Take a trip to the past in your mind or your car.
Rekindle December's embers,
Celebrate with all good reason yesterday's holidays.

Ask yourself these things as you look back.
Did the glad times outnumber the sad?
Would you change those mem'ries you pulled from Santa's sack?
Would it change the way you are today?
Would it make a difference anyway?

As you travel the roads through each past holiday,
On the highways and low bumps and byways a-stray,
Your cycle of life moved forward, up or down,
You'd keep on going through yesterday's holidays.

As this season closes on New Years Eve,
Make your glad times out-number your sad.
Promise to be good to yourself from New Year's Eve on.
You will change the way you are today.
You will make a difference all the way.
Remembering past Decembers
Helps to celebrate this season,
The holidays.

C 1997

YESTERDAY'S HOLIDAYS

BY LAURI ALLEN (A.S.C.A.P.)

61

2.

WOULD IT MAKE A DIF-F'RENCE AN-Y-WAY

(3.) AS YOU

YOU WILL MAKE A DIF-FRENCE ALL THE WAY

RE-MEM-BER-ING PAST DE-CEM-BERS HELPS TO CEL-E-BRATE THIS

SEA-SON THE HOL-I-DAYS.

WHAT IS IT?

What is it about this season
That warms the heart and soul
And gives one plenty reason
To make good will a goal?

What is it makes you want to sing
And send out thoughts of cheer
To family, friends, remembering
The ones you've missed throughout the year?

The weather's colder, snowy, wet
As Mother Nature sleeps at rest;
The warmth is not from her.
But you don't mind the winter set
Or nature's beauty still undressed,
Your heart is all astir.

Life takes on a special glow;
People seem to smile inside.
It catches you like an undertow;
You have to join the ride.

It's the love of life we feel inside
That moves us toward each other.
We have to share that love world wide
With every human brother.

December 2008

INSPIRATIONAL SONGS

(Poem) <u>YOUR HIGHER POWER</u>

CLOSE YOUR EYES

FATHER, THEY KNOW NOT WHAT THEY DO

FOR THE LOVE OF A CHILD

HAVE A LITTLE FAITH

LET THE LOVE LIGHT UP YOUR SOUL

SPIRIT CREATED IT ALL

TAKE ME ALONG WITH YOU (Take My Hand in Yours)

THANK YOU, WHOEVER YOU ARE

THE MAGIC IN YOU

THERE IS A WAY

THE TEACHER, TIME

TIME TO FORGIVE

WAKE UP HUMANITY, EVOLUTION'S HERE!

23 RD PSALM

(Poem) <u>OLD TIMES</u>

64

YOUR HIGHER POWER

When you think of where you've come to
At this time of your life...
From childhood to this year,
Recalling hopes and dreams,
Answers you'd been seeking,
Wishes that you made...
Have you sensed some higher power supporting your will
To surpass all your wishes
And suppress every fear?
It's there if you look.

And looking toward the new,
To the future of your life,
All the hopes and dreams still dormant
In the caverns of your heart,
Is there meaning to your being
Somewhere in the next decade?
It's in many a book.

Do you sense there's something higher guides you still
To pooh-pooh the superstitious
And brush away life's every tear?
Now, here's the hook...

I tell you, yes, it's very true,
Quite clear for those with ears to hear.
And to even you, without a clue...
That North Pole Genie's checking his list,
So don't screw up...
He's a perfectionist!

December 2004

CLOSE YOUR EYES

Close your eyes and think of me.
Close your eyes and you will see
Just how wise your thoughts can be
If you spend a little time just listenin'.

Close your eyes and dream a dream;
Soon you see a tiny gleam
Shining through your simple mind
If you spend a little time just dreamin'.

Close your eyes,
What a wondrous land.
Close your eyes,
And you'll understand
How it all began, this estate of man,
Close your eyes.

Close your eyes and ask the light
To brighten up your lonely night.
Just the thought that you are right
Will insure the time you spend just listenin'.

Close you eyes and you will know,
When there seems no place to go;
Turn within and ask the one
Who is there to help you keep on dreamin'.

Close your eyes,
What a wondrous land.
Close your eyes,
And you'll understand
How it all began, this estate of man,
Close your eyes; Close your eyes.
Close your eyes; close your eyes.

C 1973

66

CLOSE YOUR EYES

BY LAURI ALLEN (A.S.C.A.P.)

1. CLOSE YOUR EYES____ AND THINK OF ME____ CLOSE YOUR EYES____ AND
2. CLOSE YOUR EYES____ AND ASK THE LIGHT____ TO BRIGHT-EN UP____ YOUR

YOU WILL SEE____ JUST HOW WISE____ YOUR THOUGHTS CAN BE____ IF YOU____
LONE-LY NIGHT____ JUST THE THOUGHT____ THAT YOU____ ARE RIGHT____ WILL IN-

SPEND A LIT-TLE TIME____ JUST LIST-'NIN'____
____SURE THE TIME YOU SPEND____ JUST LIST-'NIN'____

CLOSE YOUR EYES____ AND DREAM A DREAM____ SOON YOU SEE____ A
CLOSE YOUR EYES____ NOW YOU WILL KNOW____ WHEN THERE SEEMS____ NO

TI-NY GLEAM____ SHIN-ING THROUGH YOUR SIM-PLE MIND____ IF YOU____
PLACE TO GO____ TURN WITH-IN____ AND ASK THE ONE____ WHO IS____

SPEND A LIT-TLE TIME____ JUST DREAM-IN'____
THERE TO HELP YOU KEEP____ ON DREAM-IN'____ } CLOSE YOUR____

EYES____ WHAT A WON-DROUS LAND____ CLOSE YOUR EYES____ AND YOU'LL

UN-DER- STAND HOW IT ALL BE-GAN____ THIS ES-TATE OF MAN .. CLOSE YOUR____

© 1973

67

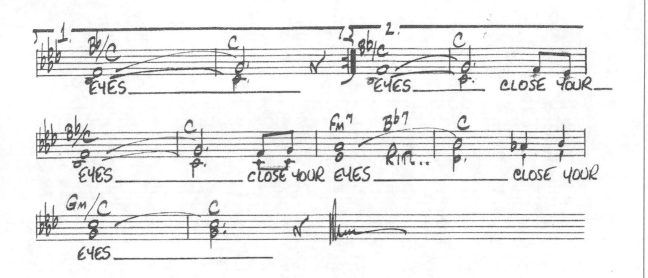

FATHER, THEY KNOW NOT WHAT THEY DO
Lyrics by Lauri Allen & Buddy Sorrel   Music by Lauri Allen

Who created the world in seven days?
And related woman to man, made them understand
'Til they learned to sin and pray?
Who planted the seed that spawned the tree
That built the cross of wood that bent him to his knees,
Oh, my Father.

Who created an earth alive with love and rich in ore
And related our dreams to schemes of hate and plans of war,
And more...
That from this ore came the hordes of screaming swords
And nails for drawing blood they drove 'til He was free?
Oh, my Father.

Who made the world full of his trials
For man to suffer through his lies for truth;
Oh, Lord, You promised Him tomorrow;
Lord, You promised Him tomorrow.
How could He know what we would do?
He cried, "Father, they know not what they do!"

Who gave us life and all we have today?
Who gave us wrong and right, dark and light
And roads to choose a way.
And for each gift he gave,
Those brave enough to follow Him alone
Were called to sacrifice by their own!

How many fathers now must die
To let their sons grow free and cry to Him;
Oh, Lord, you promised me no sorrow;
Lord, you promised me no sorrow.
But still, He died for you.

They cried, "Lord, we don't know what we're doin';
Lord, we don't know what we're doin'.
Lord, we don't know what we're doin'.

C 1972

69

FATHER, THEY KNOW NOT WHAT THEY DO

Lyrics by
LAURI ALLEN
BUDDY SORREL

Music by
LAURI ALLEN (A.S.C.A.P.)

© 1972

SUF-FER THROUGH HIS LIES___ FOR TRUTH; OH, LORD, YOU PROM-ISED HIM___ TO-
SONS GROW FREE AND CRY___ TO HIM___ OH, LORD, YOU PROM-ISED ME___ NO

-MOR-ROW_____ LORD, YOU PROM-ISED HIM___ TO-MOR-ROW___ HOW COULD HE
SOR-ROW_____ LORD, YOU PROM-ISED ME___ NO SOR-ROW___ BUT STILL I

KNOW WHAT WE WOULD DO?___ HE CRIED___ FATH-ER___ THEY KNOW NOT WHAT THEY
DIED FOR YOU _____ THEY CRIED___ LORD___ WE DON'T KNOW WHAT WE'RE

DO _____ (OH, MY)
DO-IN' _____ _____ (3.) WHO GAVE US___

FOR THE LOVE OF A CHILD

For the love of a child we sacrifice;
For a child's love our lives take on a glow.
For this love we climb mountains,
Crossing streams and canyons deep
And we toil for food and shelter
So our safety we can keep
With the love of a child deep inside.

For the love of a child we seek paradise
On this earth where we reap as we do sow.
For this love some are heroes,
Some aspire to the stars
Making life here all the better
Than we'd find on the moon or Mars
With the light of this love world wide.

This child may be wild,
May be pouty, even rowdy, even loud.
This child may be mild,
Maybe gentle or quite mentally on a cloud.

But whatever this child's worth, we'll pay the price,
Though our wars be legion, we will overthrow
Any threats to our foundation
As we travel each sojourn
Passing each initiation
To become as heaven-born
And the light of this child's love will shine
Through each one of us, our true design.

So we raise our voices high in sweetest song
For in the love of this child
We do belong all life-long.

C 2006

72

FOR THE LOVE OF A CHILD

BY LAURI ALLEN (A.S.C.A.P.)

INTRO B♭m7 · D♭7/A♭ · Dm7/G · G
FOR THE

VERSES
C · Em · F · F/G

1. LOVE___ OF A CHILD___ ┌─┐ WE SAC-RI-FICE_____ FOR A
2. LOVE___ OF A CHILD___ WE SEEK, PAR-A-DISE_____ ON THIS
3. EV-ER THIS CHILD'S WORTH___ WE'LL PAY THE PRICE_____ THOUGH OUR

C · Em · F · A7

CHILD'S LOVE OUR LIVES TAKE ON A GLOW___ FOR THIS
EARTH WHERE WE REAP AS WE DO SOW___ FOR THIS
WARS___ BE LE-GION WE WILL O-VER-THROW___ AN-Y

Dm7 · G · Cma7 · A7

LOVE___ WE CLIMB MOUN-TAINS CROSS-ING STREAMS AND CAN-YONS DEEP_AND WE
LOVE___ SOME ARE HE-ROES___ SOME AS-PIRE___ TO THE STARS___ MAK-ING
THREATS TO OUR FOUN-DA-TION___ AS WE TRAV-EL EACH SO___ JOURN PASS-ING

D7 · Dm7 · D♭ · A♭/C

TOIL FOR FOOD AND SHEL-TER SO OUR SAFE-TY WE CAN KEEP WITH THE
LIFE HERE ALL THE BET-TER THAN WE'D FIND ON THE MOON OR MARS WITH THE
EACH IN-I-TI-A-TION TO BE-COME AS HEAV-EN BORN AND THE

B♭m7 · 1. D♭7/A♭ · Dm7/G · G

LOVE___ OF A CHILD___ DEEP IN-SIDE___ (2.) FOR THE
LIGHT___ OF THIS
LIGHT OF THIS CHILD'S

2. D♭/A♭ · Gm7 · Gm7/C · F · Dm

LOVE___ WORLD-WIDE___ THIS CHILD_____ MAY BE

WILD___ MAY BE POU-TY_E-VEN ROW-DY E-VEN

LOUD___ THIS CHILD___ MAY BE MILD___

___ MAY BE GEN-TLE OR QUITE MEN-TAL-LY ON A CLOUD___

(3) BUT WHAT___

CODA

LOVE WILL SHINE___ THROUGH EACH ONE OF US___

___ OUR TRUE DE-SIGN___ SO WE RAISE OUR VOIC-ES

HIGH IN SWEET-EST SONG___ FOR IN THE LOVE OF THIS

CHILD___ WE DO___ BE - LONG___

ALL___ LIFE___ LONG___

HAVE A LITTLE FAITH

Take away your thoughts of sorrow,
Take away your evil mind.
Be afraid of only what you bring upon yourself,
And leave your fears behind.

Try believing in a way,
Lose the hate that makes you blind,
Don't believe the words of others tearing at your heart,
And see only the beauty in your mind.

And you can fly wherever you will,
And you can be whatever you wish.
You can see all the world as your own private dream,
Making it all come true
If you believe in you,
And have a little faith in Him.

Throw away fear of tomorrow,
And don't waste your heart on tears.
Be afraid of only what you bring upon yourself.
Today is not what it appears.
Think a good thought ev'ry day;
Don't turn off by all you hear;
Don't believe the words of others tearing at your heart,
'Cause the dream that you believe in is near.

And you can fly wherever you will,
And you can be whatever you wish.
You can see all the world as your own private dream,
Making it all come true
If you believe in you
And have a little faith in Him.

C 1971

75

HAVE A LITTLE FAITH

BY LAURI ALLEN (A.S.C.A.P.)

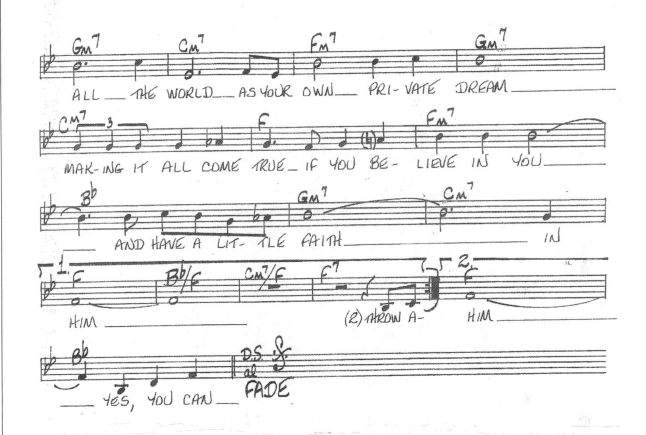

ALL THE WORLD AS YOUR OWN PRI-VATE DREAM

MAK-ING IT ALL COME TRUE IF YOU BE-LIEVE IN YOU

AND HAVE A LIT-TLE FAITH IN

HIM (2) THROW A- HIM

YES, YOU CAN FADE

LET THE LOVE LIGHT UP YOUR SOUL
(Let The Love Light Make You Whole)

Running from day to day, wandering this and that way,
There is a time you must stop and heed
And invite your soul to rest.
It will always know what's best.

There is a time when you must stop,
And holding very still, quiet your thoughts and will
And let the Love light up your soul.
Let the Love Light make you whole.

Time is only a veil, like a ship with wings full sail,
A silver curtain drawn over the drama we seed,
But if you still your mind,
Reason is there to find.

This is the time when you must stop,
And holding very still, quiet your thoughts and will
And let the Love light up your soul.
Let the Love Light make you whole.

Whole, you are being one with all,
Standing surely, living tall,
Moving daily through your highest thought,
Giving daily from your riches got
From the One, the only One.
Whole, knowing just great you are,
Creating like an avatar,
It's so easy that it seems bizarre,
Shooting farther than the highest star;
Grab the ring, that golden ring.

So completely have you turned
That a wealth of love you've earned.
Now, you know just when to stop and heed
And immerse in total mind,
Thank the Universe and find...

This is the time when you must stop,
And holding very still, quiet your thoughts and will,
And let the Love light up your soul,
Let the Love Light make you whole.
Let the Love Light make you whole.

C 2010

78

LET THE LOVE
LIGHT UP YOUR SOUL

(LET THE LOVE LIGHT MAKE YOU WHOLE)

BY LAURI ALLEN (A.S.C.A.P.)

2.

THOUGHTS AND WILL ___ AND LET THE LOVE ___ LIGHT UP YOUR SOUL ___

LET THE LOVE LIGHT ___ MAKE YOU WHOLE ___

LET THE ___ LOVE LIGHT ___ MAKE YOU WHOLE ___

WHOLE ___ YOU ARE BE-ING ONE WITH ALL ___ STAND-ING SURE-LY LIV-ING

TALL ___ MOV-ING DAIL-Y THROUGH YOUR HIGH-EST THOUGHT ___ GIV-ING DAILY FROM YOUR

RICH-ES GOT ___ FROM THE ONE ___ THE ON-LY ONE ___

WHOLE ___ KNOW-ING JUST HOW GREAT YOU ARE ___

CRE-A-TING LIKE AN AV-A-TAR ___ IT'S SO EA-SY THAT IT

SEEMS BI-ZARRE ___ SHOOT-ING FAR-THER THAN THE HIGH-EST STAR ___

GRAB THE RING ___ THAT GOLD-EN RING ___

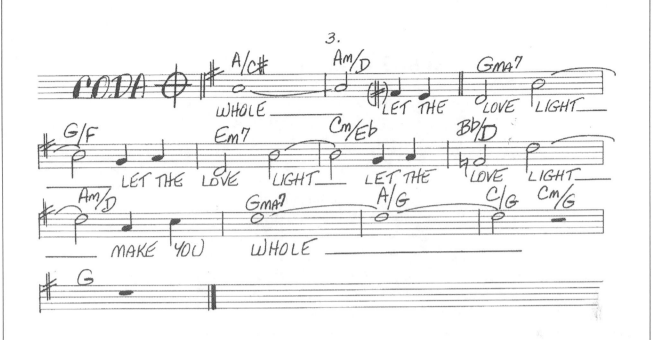

CODA

A/C# WHOLE ___

3.

Am/D (#) LET THE Gma7 LOVE LIGHT ___

G/F LET THE LOVE LIGHT ___ Em7 Cm/Eb LET THE Bb/D LOVE LIGHT ___

Am/D ___ MAKE YOU Gma7 WHOLE ___ A/G C/G Cm/G

G

SPIRIT CREATED IT ALL

Spirit makes it all happen
Makes it all here and now
Spirit can do it
The Master Creator
Never you mind just how.

For the universe, cosmos and earth,
Spirit had one great plan.
No need to ask why
Or how it began,
Yes, Spirit created man.

In the hourglass of your mind,.
Decongest your consciousness
And let the sand flow through,
To that perfect peace you find
With an attitude of pure gratitude,
Just let the love find you.
Let the love find you.

Let Spirit make it all happen
Picture your heaven on earth.
Trust in Spirit, believe it;
You know you're the artisan
And you know your own true worth.

Go within and you'll find your place
From there you will make it real;
Don't question or doubt
It all comes about
Exactly as you appeal
And Spirit, making its perfect case,
Spirit created it all.

C 2010

82

SPIRIT CREATED IT ALL

By LAURI ALLEN (A.S.C.A.P.)

1. SPIR-IT___ MAKES IT ALL HAP-PEN___ MAKES IT RIGHT
(LET) 2. SPIR-IT___ MAKE IT ALL HAP-PEN___ PIC-TURE YOUR

HERE__ AND NOW___ SPIR-IT CAN DO IT_ THE MAS-TER CRE-
HEAV-EN ON EARTH___ TRUST IN SPIR-IT_ BE-LIEVE IT_ YOU ARE A CRE-

__ A-TOR___ NEV-ER YOU MIND JUST HOW___ FOR THE
__ A-TOR___ AND YOU KNOW YOUR OWN TRUE WORTH_ GO WITH-

U-NI-VERSE COS-MOS_ AND EARTH_ SPIR-IT HAD ONE GREAT
__IN AND YOU'LL FIND_ YOUR PLACE_ FROM THERE YOU WILL MAKE IT___

PLAN___ NO NEED TO ASK WHY_ OR HOW IT BE-GAN___ THEN
REAL___ DON'T QUES-TION OR DOUBT_ IT ALL COMES A-BOUT_ EX-

SPIR-IT___ CRE-A-TED MAN___ IN THE
__ACT- LY___ AS YOU AP-

© 2010

83

TAKE ME ALONG WITH YOU
(Take My Hand In Yours)

Take my hand in yours through the longest night.
Take my hand in yours till the dawn shines bright.
And in the mornings of work and strife,
Through the afternoons of my life,
Through eternity,
Take my hand in yours.

Take my hand and lead me, be my guiding light.
Let your star precede me; let the path be right.
And when my faults and errors loom,
Lift me over loss and doom,
Till the sun, I see.
Take my hand in yours.

Take me along with you,
Flying beyond horizons far.
Take me along with you.
Let me float on high to the edge of why
With no fear or doubt, I will learn about what's true.
Take me along with you, take me along with you.

Take my hand in yours, through the tears and smiles.
Take my hand in yours as I travel miles.
And though I win or lose or what may befall,
My daily dues are paid standing tall,
And I will be free,
Take my hand in yours.

Take me along with you,
Flying beyond horizons far.
Take me along with you.
Let me float on high to the edge of why
With no fear or doubt, I will learn about what's true.
Take me along with you,
Take my hand in yours,
Take me along with you.

C 2010

TAKE ME ALONG WITH YOU
(TAKE MY HAND IN YOURS)
BY LAURI ALLEN (A.S.C.A.P.)

(1.) TAKE MY

VERSE

1. HAND IN YOURS___ THROUGH THE LONG-EST NIGHT___ TAKE MY
2. HAND AND LEAD ME__ BE MY GUID-ING LIGHT___ LET YOUR
3. HAND IN YOURS___ THROUGH THE TEARS AND SMILES___ TAKE MY

HAND IN YOURS___ TILL THE DAWN SHINES BRIGHT___ AND IN THE
STAR PRE-CEDE ME__ LET THE PATH BE RIGHT___ AND WHEN MY
HAND IN YOURS___ AS I TRA-VEL MILES___ AND THOUGH I

MORN-INGS___ OF WORK AND STRIFE___ THROUGH THE
FAULTS___ AND ER-RORS LOOM___ LIFT ME
WIN___ OR LOSE___ OR WHAT MAY BE-FALL___ MY DAIL-Y

AF-TER-NOONS___ OF MY LIFE FOR E-TER-NI-
O-VER___ LOSS AND DOOM TILL THE SUN___ I
DUES ARE PAID___ STAND-ING TALL___ AND I WILL BE

___TY___ TAKE MY HAND___ IN YOURS___ (2.) TAKE MY___

© 2010

86

2.

SEE__ TAKE MY } HAND___ IN YOURS___ TAKE ME A —
(3.) FREE__ TAKE MY }

__LONG WITH YOU___ FLY-ING BE-YOND HO-RI-ZONS FAR__ TAKE ME A—

__LONG WITH YOU___ LET ME FLOAT ON HIGH TO THE EDGE OF WHY WITH NO

FEAR OR DOUBT I WILL LEARN A-BOUT WHAT'S TRUE___

TAKE ME A-LONG WITH YOU___ TAKE ME A- LONG WITH YOU___

(3.) TAKE MY___

CODA

___ TAKE MY HAND IN YOURS___ TAKE ME A—

__ LONG__ WITH YOU.___

THANK YOU WHOEVER YOU ARE

Thanks for the sunlight and rain and snow;
They help Mother Earth to flourish and grow.
These are the seasons of life we know.
Thank you, Whoever you are.

Thanks for the mountains and land below,
For oceans abound and winds that blow.
This is the home of love we know.
Thank you, Whoever you are.

Who you are is great and good,
Maybe just misunderstood.
Love and power fill your neighborhood where you are.
Who you are is light and life
And your laws cut like a knife,
But we follow with faith like a wife
Wherever, Whoever you are.

And we say thank you,
We know that you care
When we turn to you in all our despair,
Seeking love no one else will share,
You're there,
Wherever, Whoever you are,
Thank you.

C 1995

THANK YOU
WHOEVER YOU ARE

BY LAURI ALLEN (A.S.C.A.P.)

2.

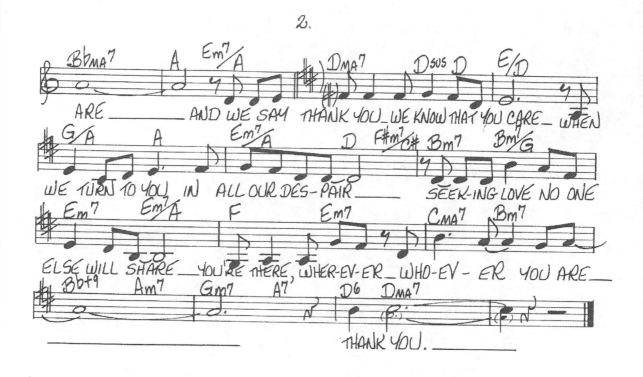

Bbma7	A	Em7/A	Dma7	Dsus D	E/D

ARE _____ AND WE SAY THANK YOU_ WE KNOW THAT YOU CARE_ WHEN

G/A	A	Em7/A	D F#m7/C# Bm7	Bm/G

WE TURN TO YOU IN ALL OUR DES-PAIR _____ SEEK-ING LOVE NO ONE

Em7	Em7/A	F	Em7	Cma7	Bm7

ELSE WILL SHARE ___ YOU'RE THERE, WHER-EV-ER __ WHO-EV- ER YOU ARE__

Bb+9	Am7	Gm7	A7	D6 Dma7

_____   THANK YOU. _____

THE MAGIC IN YOU

The magic in you is more than the sky,
Is more than a star falling from high;
It's more than before man.
The magic in you is richer than gold,
Is stronger than olove and longer than old
In fortune's plan.

The magic in you is music to play;
It's song begins each day
And lights every dark night.

You know that it's real, as real as the rain,
And laughs at the sun and pleasure and pain
Throughout life's span.

The world is aglow
From the spark you create
In a dark and a fated and dated and latent heart.

The magic in you is no mystery.
It's more than the real of what you can see,
More than a miracle could be.
It's more than a miracle could be.

C 1966 – 2010

THE MAGIC IN YOU

BY LAURI ALLEN (A.S.C.A.P.)

THERE IS A WAY

There is a way to be all you want to be.
There is a way to see all you want to see.
There is a way to reach the stars,
And use the sun and moon to light your heart.
There is a way to turn your life around
And sing a brand-new tune at each day's start.

The way is inward;
It's a circle back to you.
The way is inward
And another circle to the one who made you,
The one who loves you ,
The one whose work is never done,
The one who keeps you one-on-one with the greatest One,
There is a way.

There is a way to know the world as your toy.
There is a way to show all your love and joy.
There is a way to travel sky and ground
And feel the wind and rain fresh on your face.
There is a way to know when you have found
You haven't sought in vain your special place,

The way is inward;
It's a circle back to you.
The way is inward
And another circle to the one who made you,
The one who loves you,
The one whose work is never done,
The one who keeps you one-on-one with the greatest One,
There is a way; there is a way.
The way is inward; there is a way.

C 1986

94

THERE IS A WAY

BY LAURI ALLEN (A.S.C.A.P.)

VERSE 1.

THERE IS A WAY___ TO BE___ ALL YOU WANT TO BE___

___ THERE IS A WAY___ TO SEE ALL YOU WANT TO SEE___ THERE IS A

WAY___ TO REACH THE STARS___ AND USE THE SUN___ AND MOON___ TO LIGHT YOUR
(2) WAY___ TO TRAVEL SKY AND GROUND___ AND FEEL THE WIND AND RAIN___ FRESH ON YOUR

HEART___ THERE IS A WAY___ TO TURN YOUR LIFE A-___ROUND___ AND SING A
FACE___ THERE IS A WAY___ TO KNOW WHEN YOU HAVE FOUND___ YOU HAVE-N'T

BRAND-NEW TUNE AT EACH DAY'S START___ THE WAY IS___
SOUGHT IN VAIN YOUR SPE-CIAL PLACE___

CHORUS

IN-WARD___ IT'S A CIR-CLE BACK TO YOU___ THE WAY IS IN-WARD___ AND AN-

© 1986

95

2.

_ OTH-ER CIR-CLE TO THE ONE WHO MADE YOU _ THE ONE WHO LOVES YOU _ THE ONE WHOSE

WORK IS NEV-ER DONE _ THE ONE WHO KEEPS YOU ONE-ON-ONE WITH THE GREAT-EST

ONE _____ THERE IS A _____ WAY _____

_____ (2.) THERE IS A _____ WAY _ TO KNOW _ THE WORLD _ AS YOUR TOY ___

_____ THERE IS A ___ WAY _ TO SHOW ALL YOUR LOVE AND JOY _____

_____ THERE IS A ____

3

97

THE TEACHER TIME

There is a time to work,
A time to live and play awhile.
The Teacher, Time will tell you when you've had enough,
It's time to rest awhile.

There is a time to kiss,
A time to speak of stars above.
This precious time to kiss and speak of stars above
Will teach your heart to love.

Time is the teacher
Of all that life can offer.
Just use this feature to elevate your dreams.

The moment when you miss
That moment you saw stars on high
Is when the teacher feels the lesson's learned,
Life is earned
And you know why.

Time will remind you
Of what has passed you by.
And you'll remember with a sigh,
And say good bye.
And you'll remember with a sigh,
And say good bye.

C 1966-2010

THE TEACHER TIME

BY LAURI ALLEN (A.S.C.A.P.)

THERE IS A TIME TO WORK___ A TIME TO LIVE AND PLAY A-WHILE___

THE TEACH-ER TIME WILL TELL YOU WHEN YOU'VE HAD E-NOUGH...IT'S TIME TO REST A-WHILE___

THERE IS A TIME TO KISS___ A TIME TO SPEAK OF STARS A-BOVE___

THIS PRE-CIOUS TIME TO KISS AND SPEAK OF STARS A-BOVE WILL TEACH YOUR HEART TO LOVE___

TIME IS THE TEACH-ER___ OF ALL THAT LIFE CAN OFF - ER___

JUST USE THIS FEA-TURE___ TO EL-E-VATE YOUR DREAMS.___

THE MO-MENT WHEN YOU MISS___ THAT MO-MENT YOU SAW STARS ON HIGH___

Cm7   F7   Cm   F7

IS   WHEN THE TEACH-ER FEELS THE LES-SON'S LEARNED___ LIFE IS EARNED AND

Bb   Bb7   Eb   Cm/F

YOU KNOW WHY___   TIME WILL RE-MIND YOU___   OF WHAT HAS

Bb   F   F7

PASSED YOU BY___ AND YOU'LL RE-MEM-BER WITH A SIGH___ AND SAY GOOD-

Gm7   Gm/C   F   F7

___ BYE___   AND YOU'LL RE-MEM-BER WITH A SIGH___ AND SAY GOOD-

Db Eb/C   Bb

___ BYE_____

TIME TO FORGIVE

Time to forgive,
Let go and live your life.
Love is the key that opens the door
To free your soul to fly and explore.

Time to forgive.
Release the pain and strife.
Move into joy and let your voice ring
That song hiding in you wants you to sing.

It's a good time to let go of worry.
It's a good day to smile through your tears.
Whatever your fears, your worries or woes,
Release them to nothingness,
Let that door close.
It's a good time, the right time to forgive.

Time to be joyful,
Let go of anger and doubt.
Throw them out and let your light shine.
Time to feel whole, complete and divine.

It's a good time to let go of worry.
It's a good day to smile through your tears.
Whatever your fears, your worries or woes,
Release them to nothingness,
let that door close.
It's a good time, the right time,
A good time, the right time,
It's time to forgive.

C 2010

TIME TO FORGIVE

BY LAURI ALLEN (A.S.C.A.P.)

THROUGH YOUR TEARS_ WHAT-EV-ER YOUR FEARS_YOUR WOR-RIES OR WOES_ RE-
LEASE THEM TO NOTH-ING-NESS LET THAT DOOR CLOSE_ IT'S A GOOD TIME_ THE
RIGHT TIME TO FOR- GIVE _____

CODA
RIGHT TIME_ A GOOD TIME_ THE RIGHT TIME_ IT'S
TIME__ TO_ FOR- GIVE _____

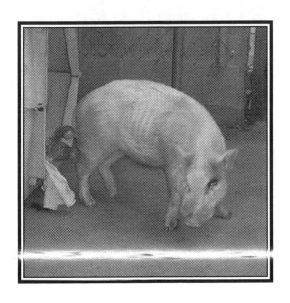

WAKE UP HUMANITY, EVOLUTION'S HERE!

Wake up, humanity, evolution is coming.
Listen just a little harder for the song it sings
And the joy it brings
To each soul whose heart is open wide,
Letting all the beauty flow inside.
Pretty soon, you're dancing on a cloud,
Singing right out loud
Evolution's song, pulling you along.

Wake up, humanity, evolution is calling,
A message intense with ardor that you must understand;
You are one with all at your command.
Let the joy of it carry you on high,
Spirit tells you believe, yes, it is nigh.
And then, you feel it, deep inside,
Are you satisfied?
Evolution's here; now there is no fear.
Evolution's here.

Why are you waiting to wake up your soul?
Stop hesitating, you're not on parole.
You're free to take control of your life.
Throw out the fear, the doubt and the strife.
You are Spirit's child created singly and self-styled,
One of a kind, a master-mind.

Wake up, humanity; evolution has caught up.
It's the principle blooming everywhere and you must prepare
To step up and take charge, if you dare
To become as the one who created all;
It's your turn to be ready to take the call,
Evolution's calling, calling you now to sing along
Evolution's song.

Sing it loud and clear;
Wake up, humanity,
Evolution's here.
Wake up, humanity,
Evolution's here.

C 2010

WAKE UP HUMANITY EVOLUTION 'S HERE!

BY LAURI ALLEN (A.S.C.A.P.)

VERSE 1.
WAKE UP HU-MAN-I-TY___ EV-O-LU-TION IS COM-ING___
LIS-TEN JUST A LIT-TLE HARD-ER FOR___ THE SONG___ IT___ SINGS___ AND THE
JOY___ IT___ BRINGS___ TO EACH SOUL WHOSE HEART IS O-PEN WIDE LET-TING
ALL THE BEAU-TY FLOW IN-SIDE___ PRET-TY SOON YOU'RE DAN-CING ON A CLOUD SING-ING
RIGHT___ OUT___ LOUD___ EV-O-LU-TION'S SONG___
PULL-ING YOU A-LONG___

VERSE 2-3
(2) WAKE UP___ HU-MAN-I-TY___ EV-O-LU-TION___ IS CALL-ING___ A
(3) WAKE UP___ HU-MAN-I-TY___ EV-O-LU-TION HAS CAUGHT UP___ IT'S THE

© 2010

105

2

SING IT LOUD AND CLEAR ——— WAKE UP HU-

-MAN-I-TY ——— EV-O-LU-TION'S HERE ———

—— WAKE UP HU-MAN-I-TY ——— EV-O-LU-TION'S HERE—

WAKE UP!

23 RD PSALM
(Traditional)

The Lord is my shepherd, I shall not want.
He makes me lie down in green pastures.
He leads me beside still waters;
He restores my soul,
Restores my soul.

He leads me in the path of righteousness for His name's sake.
Yea, though I walk through the valley of the shadow of death,
I will fear no evil for He is with me
His rod and staff,
They comfort me.

He prepares a table before me in the presence of my enemies.
He annoints my head with oil
And my cup runs over,
My cup runs over.

Oh, surely, goodness and mercy shall follow me
All of the days of my life.
And I shall dwell in the house of the Lord,
And I shall dwell in the house of the Lord forever;
Yes I shall dwell in the house of the Lord forever,
Forever, forever.

C 1973 rev. 1976

23 RD PSALM

Music by LAURI ALLEN (A.S.C.A.P.)

OLD TIMES

Nothing is as sweet as memories and old friends.
Nothing's quite as dear as reliving time's old trends,
Those of younger, eager days and nights
Spent laughing, crying, getting through
Our youthful joys and fights!

We know, don't we...
What was real back then
And what is true right now?
We know, don't we...
What we did and who we were back when
We made our marks and took our bow?

Old times, old times,
Make way for new
And soften every blow life deals
To me and you.

Somehow, now looms larger than recalling what is past.
We are who we are today 'cause we got through it all as last.
And down the road, as we move on,
Our children look back too,
Telling stories, songs and jokes of ours,
As if they were new.

They will never know, first hand,
How full of life we were,
Tasting every day's buffet
And drunk on life's liqueur.

They'll create their own "Old Times,"
Sweeter for them now
Than when ours were going strong.
They'll look back and know, as we,
That now's where they belong.

Old times, old times,
Make way for new
And soften every blow life deals
To me and you...
And all our children too.

December 2000

111